Half Ba Harvest Cookbook for Beginners

2021 Cookbook Harness the full power of meals with super quick, super easy and enjoyable recipes for easy weight loss.Instant, meal-ready, meal-ready and easy-to-make recipes

The information in the following pages is broadly considered a truthful and accurate account of facts and as such, any inattention, use, or misuse of the information in question by the reader will render any resulting actions solely under their purview. There are no scenarios in which the publisher or the original author of this work can be in any fashion deemed liable for any hardship or damages that may befall them after undertaking information described herein.

Additionally, the information in the following pages is intended only for informational purposes and should thus be thought of as universal. As befitting its nature, it is presented without assurance regarding its prolonged validity or interim quality. Trademarks that are mentioned are done without written consent and can in no way be considered an endorsement from the trademark holder.

TABLE OF CONTENTS

BREAKFAST

Molasses Breadsticks

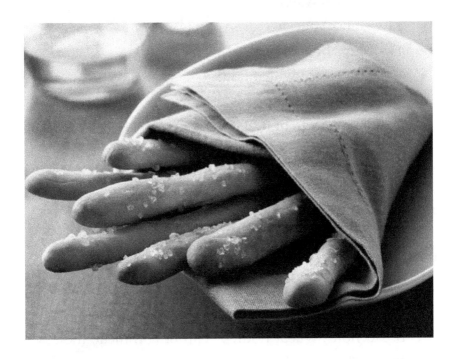

Preparation Time: 20 minutes

Cooking Time: 18 minutes

Servings: 12

Ingredients

- 2 tablespoons brown sugar
- 1 cup warm water
- 1 (¼-ounce) package dry yeast
- 1½-2 cups bread flour
- 1½ cups whole-wheat flour
- ½ cup plus 2 tablespoons cornmeal
- 2 tablespoons light molasses
- 2 tablespoons butter, melted
- 2 eggs
- 1½ teaspoons salt
- 1 tablespoon cold water

Directions

1. For breadsticks: in the bowl of a stand mixer, dissolve brown sugar and yeast in warm water. Add ½ cup of bread flour, wheat flour, ½ cup of cornmeal, molasses, butter, 1 egg and salt and beat on medium speed until smooth. Add enough remaining bread flour and beat until a dough form.

2. Arrange the dough onto a floured surface and with your hands, knead until smooth and elastic. Now, transfer the dough into a well-greased bowl and turn to coat. With a

plastic wrap, cover the bowl and set aside in a warm place for about 1 hour.

3. With your hands, punch the dough down. Arrange the dough onto a floured surface and cut into 12 pieces. Shape each dough piece into 9x½-inch breadsticks. Arrange the breadsticks onto greased baking sheets about 2-inch apart. With a plastic wrap, cover each baking sheet and set aside in warm place for about 20-30 minutes. Prepare the oven and adjust the heat at 375 degrees.

4. For egg wash: Stir egg and 1 tablespoon of cold water. Coat the breadsticks with egg mixture and sprinkle with cornmeal.

5. Bake for about 13-18 minutes or until top becomes golden brown.

6. Take out from the oven and transfer the baking sheets onto wire racks to cool completely.

Nutrition: 177 Calories 3.2g Total Fat 4.8g Protein 31g Carbs

Grilled Tomato

Preparation Time: 5 minutes

Cooking Time: 20 minutes

Serving: 2

Ingredients:

- 2 Tomatoes
- herbs
- pepper

Directions:

1. Wash the tomatoes and cut them in half. Spray pepper over bot h sides of tomatoes and sprinkle your favorite herbs, be it parsley, oregano, basil, rosemary, sage, etc.
2. Place the tomatoes in the tray and put them in air fryer at a temperature of 160-degree for 20 minutes. Check the tomatoes according to your taste and if they are not done give them a bit more heat. Serve them your favorite herbs or cheese.

Nutrition: 27 Calories 8g Fat

Pancakes

Preparation Time: 5 minutes

Cooking Time: 5 minutes

Servings: 4

Ingredients:

- 1 egg
- 1 banana
- Honey, Nutella, caramel (optional)

Directions:

1. Put an egg in a bowl. Mash a banana in it. When it is fully mashed. Spray some oil in air fryer basket.
2. Set the temperature for 5 minutes at 200 degrees Wait for 5 minutes, when it is fully golden.
3. Shift it to a plate and put your favorite spread or honey on it.

Nutrition: 90 calories 14g fats 3g fiber

Sauces Egg and Cheese

Preparation Time: 4 minutes

Cooking Time: 7 minutes

Servings: 4

Ingredients:

- Sausage Patties
- Egg
- Cheese
- Air fryer safe bowl
- Buns or slices

Directions:

1. Put the patties in air fryer and set the temperature at 200 degrees for 5 minutes.
2. Cut the bun from half and put the cheese slices on to it. Put it in the air fryer for 3 minutes at 300 degrees.
3. Put the oil in an air fryer safe bowl and put the beaten egg in it with some pepper and salt mixed in it. Put the bowl in the air fryer for three minutes at 360 degrees.
4. Tip: if you have a rack put all three things in the air fryer at 3600 degrees for 3 minutes, then take out the buns and set a timer for another three minutes.
5. Put the egg on the half bun and sausage on the other half.
6. Now put them all together and enjoy your breakfast.

Nutrition: 101 calories 12g fats 3g fiber

Cheese Sandwiches

Preparation Time: 3 minutes

Cooking Time: 7 minutes

Servings: 2

Ingredients:

- 2 bread slices
- ½ cup Mozzarella cheese
- 1 slice American cheddar cheese
- 1 tbsp Butter

Directions:

1. Microwave the butter for 20 seconds. Preheat air fryer on 200 degrees for 5 minutes. Brush melted butter on the slices. Put cheddar cheese on the opposite sides of the slices.
2. Add mozzarella cheese on it. Take the other slice and put it on the slice with cheddar and mozzarella cheese. Put it in the air fryer basket.
3. Set the timer for 200 degrees for 7 minutes. Take it out and serve it with any sauce or paste you like.

Nutrition: 170 calories 11g fats 3g protein

Breakfast Souffle

Preparation Time: 10 minutes

Cooking Time: 5 minutes

Servings: 4

Ingredients:

- 4 Eggs
- Red chili pepper
- Parsley
- 4 tbsp Light cream

Directions:

1. Firstly, take parsley and chili and chopped them finely. Take a bowl, place the eggs in it and mix it in the pepper parsley and cream.
2. Now take the egg mixture fill the dishes almost half with it. Just for 8 minutes bake the soufflés at 200°C.
3. In case you have to serve the soufflés beaux (soft), the cooking time of 5 minutes is sufficient.

Nutrition: 98 calories 11g fats 1g fiber

Egg in a Whole

Preparation Time: 10 minutes

Cooking Time: 5 minutes

Servings: 2

Ingredients

- 2 Bread slices
- Butter
- 2 eggs.

Directions:

1. Preheat the air fryer at 360 degrees for 5 minutes.' Brush butter on the pan. Take a slice and cut a circle in the middle using a glass.
2. Then repeat for the second too. Put the slices on the butter. Put an egg in the center of each slice.
3. Set the timer for 5 minutes at 360 degrees. Change the side of the slice. Serve it with your favorite herbs or black pepper.

Nutrition: 77 calories 12g fats 3g protein

Breakfast Potatoes

Preparation Time: 5 minutes

Cooking Time: 15 minutes

Servings: 4

Ingredients:

- 2 potatoes
- A tomato
- An onion
- Pepper

Directions:

1. Wash the potatoes and peel them or do not peel them as you wish. Cut the potatoes into cubes and put them in air fryer and spray some oil Put them for 10 minutes at the temperature of 400 degrees.
2. Take out the basket and put some chopped onion and tomatoes. Spray some more oil. Put them for 15 more minutes at the same temperature. Take them out on a plate.
3. Sprinkle some pepper on it and serve them.

Nutrition: 101 calories 11g fats 4g protein

Air Fried Gourmet Potato Chips

Preparation Time: 10 minutes

Cooking Time: 50 minutes

Servings: 4

Ingredients:

- 1 kg Potatoes
- 1 tbsp Duck fat
- Maldon salt

Directions:

1. Wash the potatoes properly and peel them. Slice them thinly. Place in a large bowl of cold water, which would release the starch of potatoes and make them crispier than ever before.
2. Heat the duck fat for 2 minutes. Strain the potato water and make them dry.
3. Add it to the Air fryer basket and cook for 40-50 minutes. Transfer to a bowl and sprinkle Maldon salt. Serve hot and warm.

Nutrition: 201 Calories 3.1g Fat

APPETIZER AND SIDES

Parsley Squash Mix

Preparation Time: 10 minutes

Cooking Time: 45 minutes

Servings: 4

Ingredients:

- 2 tablespoons olive oil
- 1 spaghetti squash, seedless and halved
- Salt and ground black pepper, to taste
- 2 garlic cloves, peeled and minced
- 1 tablespoon fresh parsley, chopped
- 1 tablespoon fresh basil, chopped
- 3 tablespoons pine nuts

Directions:

1. Put squash halves on a lined baking sheet, bake in the oven at 350ºF for 40 minutes, scrape the squash and put it in a bowl. Heat a pan with the oil over medium-high heat, add the garlic, squash and the rest of the ingredients, toss, cook for 5 minutes, divide between plates and serve as a side dish.

Nutrition: 162 Calories 8g Fat 2g Fiber 16g Carbs 4g Protein

Basil Zucchini Mix

Preparation Time: 10 minutes

Cooking Time: 5 minutes

Servings: 4

Ingredients:

- 3 zucchinis, spiralized
- 1 cup basil leaves
- A pinch of salt and black pepper
- ½ tablespoon olive oil
- 1 cup spinach
- 2 garlic cloves, peeled and minced
- 1 avocado, pitted and peeled
- ⅓ cup cashews, roasted
- Juice and zest of 1 lime

Directions:

1. Heat a pan with the oil over medium-high heat, add the zucchini noodles, stir, and cook for 4 minutes. In a food processor, mix the basil with salt and the rest of the ingredients and pulse well. Combine the zucchinis with the basil mix, toss and serve.

Nutrition: 200 Calories 4g Fat 4g Fiber 10g Carbs 8g Protein

Green Beans Mix

Preparation Time: 10 minutes

Cooking Time: 10 minutes

Servings: 4

Ingredients:

- 4 tomatoes, cored and sliced
- 2 garlic cloves, minced
- ½ cup almonds, toasted and sliced
- 1-pound green beans, trimmed
- 1 tablespoon olive oil
- 1 tablespoon parsley, chopped
- Salt and ground black pepper, to taste

Directions:

1. Heat a pan with the olive oil over medium-high heat, add the garlic, stir, and cook for 1 minute. Add the green beans and the rest of the ingredients, cook for 8-9 minutes more, divide between plates and serve.

Nutrition: 140 Calories 2g Fat 6g Fiber 12g Carbs 5g Protein

Red Potato Salad

Preparation Time: 15 minutes

Cooking Time: 15-20 minutes

Servings: 4-5

Ingredients:

- 6-7 medium sized red potatoes, scrubbed and cut into pieces
- 1 cup mayonnaise
- ½ tablespoon brown mustard
- ¾ teaspoon white vinegar
- ¾ teaspoon celery salt
- 4 hardboiled eggs, roughly chopped
- 1 to 2 celery stalks, thinly sliced
- ¾ cup onions, sliced
- 4 slices of bacon, cooked and crumbled
- Salt and pepper to taste
- Freshly chopped chives for garnishing

Directions:

1. Put the potato chunks in a medium sized sauce pan and then cover with cold water. Bring to a boil over medium high heat. After the potatoes have boiled, reduce the heat to medium low and continue to cook for 8 to 10 minutes until they are tender. Drain the potatoes and then set it aside. In a separate large bowl, combine the mayonnaise, mustard, vinegar, celery salt, eggs, onions, bacon and

celery. Mix all the ingredients well and then finally add the potatoes. Season to taste with salt and pepper. Chill the salad over night or for at least 2 hours, and garnish with chives before serving.

Nutrition: Calories: 296 Fat: 123g Fiber: 6g Carbs: 31g Protein: 6 g

Crispy Fried Okra

Preparation Time: 10 minutes

Cooking Time: 15-20 minutes

Servings: 3-4

Ingredients:

- 10 pods of okra
- 1 cup cornmeal
- ¼ teaspoon ground pepper
- ½ cup vegetable oil
- ¼ teaspoon salt
- 1 egg
- Kosher salt and white pepper vinegar, for serving

Directions:

1. Beat the egg in a large bowl, and soak the okra in it for 10 minutes. In another, medium sized bowl, combine salt, pepper, and cornmeal. Heat oil in a large skillet over medium high heat. Dip the okra in the cornmeal mixture, coating it evenly on all sides. Place okra in the hot oil, reduce the heat to medium low as the okra starts to turn brown. Stir continuously. Drain on paper towels, and serve with salt and pepper vinegar.

Nutrition: Calories: 250 Fat: 10g Fiber: 5g Carbs: 22.5g Protein: 4g

LUNCH

Peppercorn Short Ribs

Preparation Time: 10 Minutes

Cooking Time: 4 Hours

Servings: 8

Ingredients:

- 4 lbs. short ribs, bone-in
- Eight peppercorns
- 2 cups low-sodium beef
- One onion, diced
- Two carrots, peeled, diced
- Two celery stalks, diced
- Four cloves, minced
- 1 tsp thyme
- 1 tsp rosemary
- Two bay leaves
- 2 tsp salt
- 2 tsp black pepper
- Extra virgin olive oil

Directions:

1. Heat extra virgin olive oil in a skillet. Add onions and garlic, and sauté until brown.

2. Place onion mixture in a slow cooker, add short ribs, carrots, celery stalk, cloves, thyme, rosemary, peppercorns, bay leaves, salt, and black pepper.
3. Cook on high for 4 hours.

Nutrition: Calories 520 Carbs 3.7 g Fat 24 g Protein 67 g Sodium 923 mg

Spicy Italian Sausage and Zucchini Noodles

Preparation Time: 20 Minutes

Cooking Time: 4 Hours

Servings: 6

Ingredients:

- 6 Spicy Italian pork sausages
- One onion, peeled and diced
- 2 cups low-sodium chicken stock
- One tomato, diced
- Four zucchinis, peeled
- 1 tsp oregano
- 1 tsp salt
- 1 tsp black pepper
- Extra virgin olive oil

Directions:

1. Coat slow cooker with a little extra virgin olive oil, and set to high.
2. Slice sausage into ½" thick rounds, and place in a slow cooker.
3. Heat 3 tbsp extra virgin olive oil in a skillet, add onion and garlic, sauté for a minute, and add to slow cooker.
4. Add tomatoes, oregano, and a tsp of salt and black pepper along with the chicken stock, cover, and cook for 4 hours.

5. Using Mandolin, slice zucchini vertically to create thin Zucchini Noodles.

6. Top zucchini noodles with Spicy Italian Sausage and serve.

Nutrition: Calories 254 Carbs 8.5 g Fat 14 g Protein 24 g Sodium 1044 mg

Meaty Cauliflower Lasagna

Preparation Time: 20 Minutes

Cooking Time: 5 Hours

Servings: 8

Ingredients:

- 1 lb. ground beef
- One small cauliflower head
- One red onion, diced
- Four cloves garlic, minced
- 2 cups crushed tomato
- 1 cup Mozzarella, shredded
- One egg
- 1 tsp oregano
- One bay leaf
- 1 tsp black pepper
- 1 tsp salt
- Extra virgin olive oil

Directions:

1. Brush slow cooker with olive oil, and set the slow cooker on medium-high.
2. Separate cauliflower into florets, peel the outer layer of cauliflower stem and dice stem.
3. Place cauliflower in the food processor, pulse into rice-like granules, crack an egg into cauliflower, and mix along with ½ tsp of salt.

4. Place 3 tbsp olive oil in a skillet, add ground beef, brown, add crushed tomatoes, oregano, bay leaf, black pepper, and ½ tsp salt, mix.
5. Place ½ cauliflower mixture in a slow cooker, next layer 1/3 of the beef mixture and ½ of cheese, place remaining cauliflower on top.
6. Spoon remaining sauce on top of the cauliflower, sprinkle with remaining cheese.
7. Cook on medium-high for 5 hours.

Nutrition: Calories 342 Carbs 8.2 g Fat 14 g Protein 45 g Sodium 681 mg

Chili Verde

Preparation Time: 10 Minutes

Cooking Time: 7 Hours

Servings: 8

Ingredients:

- 1½ lbs. pork shoulder
- ½ lb. sirloin, cubed
- 4 Anaheim chiles, stemmed
- Six cloves garlic, minced
- ½ cup cilantro, chopped
- Two onions, peeled and sliced
- Two tomatoes, chopped.
- 1 tbsp tomato paste
- One lime
- 1 tbsp cumin
- 1 tbsp oregano
- Extra virgin olive oil

Directions:

1. Slice pork shoulder into ½" cubes, and set slow cooker to medium. Heat oil in a frying pan, add onions, Anaheim chilies, garlic, and sauté for 2 minutes.
2. Place skillet mixture into a slow cooker, add pork shoulder, sirloin, and stir.
3. Add tomatoes, cilantro, tomato paste, cumin, oregano, and salt to the pot.

4. Cover and cook for 7 hours.

5. Squeeze a little lime in each bowl when serving.

Nutrition: Calories 262 Carbs 6 g Fat 16 g Protein 23 g Sodium 63 mg

DINNER

Rosemary Buttered Pork Chops

Preparation Time: 5 Minutes

Cooking Time: 20 Minutes

Servings: 4

Ingredients:

- ½ tbsp. olive oil
- 2 tbsp. butter
- 1 tbsp. rosemary
- Four pork chops
- Salt and black pepper to taste
- Pinch of paprika
- ½ tsp. chili powder

Directions:

1. Rub the pork chops with olive oil, salt, black pepper, paprika, and chili powder. Heat a grill to medium, add the pork chops and cook for 10 minutes, flipping once halfway through.

2. Remove to a serving plate. In a pan over low heat, warm the butter until it turns a nutty brown. Pour over the pork chops, sprinkle with rosemary, and serve.

Nutrition: Calories 363 Fat 21.4 g Carbs 3.8 g Protein 38.5 g

Beef Tenderloin

Preparation Time: 15 Minutes

Cooking Time: 15 Minutes

Servings: 4

Ingredients:

- 6 tbsp. Butter, salted, softened & divided
- 2 Garlic cloves, minced finely
- 4 oz. Mushrooms, chopped finely
- 1 tbsp. Avocado Oil
- 1 1/2 lbs. Beef Tenderloin Steaks, sliced
- Salt & Pepper, as needed

Directions:

1. First, spoon in two tablespoons of butter to a heated saucepan over medium-high heat.
2. Once the butter has melted, stir in the mushrooms.
3. Cook them for 4 minutes or until they are golden brown.
4. Now, stir in the garlic, salt, and pepper to it and sauté for a minute.
5. Move the mushrooms to a plate and set it aside.
6. With a fork, coat the mushrooms with the left butter.
7. After that, keep the butter in waxed paper and roll it into a log by wrapping it up. Chill it until it needs to be used.
8. Keep the steaks at room temperature about 2 hours before it is being cooked.

9. Then, take a large saucepan over medium-high heat, and to this, pour the oil.

10. When the oil is heated, stir in the steaks and cook for 5 minutes per side. Tip: If it is thicker, more time is needed.

11. Take the pan from heat and set it aside for 3 minutes or until the meat's internal temperature reaches 140F to 150F.

12. Serve warm with the chilled butter on top.

Nutrition: Calories: 406Kcal Carbohydrates: 2.3g Fat: 24.1g Proteins: 38.1g

Buttered Chicken with Brussels Sprouts

Preparation Time: 5 Minutes

Cooking Time: 30 Minutes

Servings: 4

Ingredients:

- 8 Chicken Breasts
- Three cloves of Garlic cloves,
- minced finely
- 1 lb. Brussels sprouts,
- whole or sliced into half
- ¾ cup Chicken Broth
- ½ tsp. Sea Salt
- 2 tsp. Butter, preferably grass-fed
- ¼ tsp. Black Pepper

Directions:

1. Start by placing the chicken pieces in a heated, large saucepan over medium-high heat.
2. Now, spoon in salt and pepper over it. Sear it for 3 to 4 minutes or until the chicken is cooked and is slightly browned at the bottom.
3. Turn them over and top it with salt and pepper. Cook for a few minutes.
4. Put the cooked chicken to a plate and add the brussels sprouts to the pan.

5. Next, pour the chicken stock into it and allow it to simmer for about 10 minutes.
6. Return the chicken pieces to the heat and cook for a few minutes or until the chicken is fully cooked.
7. Finally, stir in the butter and garlic to the pan. Sauté the garlic for 2 minutes or until aromatic.
8. Spoon the garlic butter over the top of the chicken and brussels sprouts. Coat well and stir.
9. Transfer to the serving bowl and serve it hot. Garnish it with black pepper.

Nutrition: Calories: 446Kcal Carbohydrates: 8g Fat: 15.1 Proteins: 63.7g

Pork Stir-Fry

Preparation Time: 5 Minutes

Cooking Time: 20 Minutes

Servings: 4

Ingredients:

- 10 oz. Broccoli florets
- 2 tbsp. Sesame Oil
- 1 Carrot, sliced thinly into sticks
- 2 tbsp. Tamari
- 1 lb. Pork Tenderloin, sliced
- 2 Garlic cloves, minced
- ½ tsp. Ginger, fresh & minced

Directions:

1. First, spoon in the one tablespoon of oil to a large saucepan and heat it over medium-high heat.
2. Once the oil becomes hot, stir in the pork and cook for 6 minutes or until browned.
3. Then, pour the rest of the oil into the pan over high heat.
4. After that, add garlic and stir for 30 seconds or until fragrant.
5. Now, stir in the broccoli to it and mix well.
6. Continue cooking for 5 minutes or until tender and softened. Cover for further 2
7. minutes while keeping it covered.

8. Finally, return the pork to the pan and spoon in ginger and tamari sauce. Stir until the vegetables are prepared to your desire continuously.

Nutrition: Calories: 247Kcal Carbohydrates: 8g Fat: 12g Fiber: 3g Saturated Fat: 2g Sugar: 3g Proteins: 27g Sodium: 326m

Cauliflower Chowder

Preparation Time: 5 Minutes

Cooking Time: 25 Minutes

Servings: 4

Ingredients:

- 1 tbsp. Butter, preferably grass-fed
- 1 Cauliflower head, torn into florets
- ½ cup Onion, finely diced
- 1 ½ cups Vegetable Stock
- Five cloves of Garlic, finely minced
- ½ cup Carrots, diced
- Salt, to taste
- ¼ cup Cream cheese
- 1 tsp. Pepper, grounded freshly
- ½ tsp. Oregano, dried
- Olive Oil, as required

Directions:

1. Start by heating a Dutch oven medium heat, and stir in butter, onions, and garlic.
2. Cook for 4 minutes or wait until the onions are softened.
3. Next, stir in carrots, pepper, cauliflower, oregano, vegetable broth, and salt to the Dutch oven.
4. Bring the mixture to a boil and allow it to simmer. Reduce heat.

5. Simmer for 15 minutes or until the cauliflower is soft & cooked.
6. Remove from heat. With an immersion blender, blend the soup partly.
7. Now, return the soup to the stove. Pour a cup of broth along with the cream cheese.
8. Combine.
9. Simmer for further 10 minutes. Drizzle with olive oil and serve it hot.

Nutrition: Calories: 130Kcal Carbohydrates: 10g Fat: 7g Proteins: 5g

Chicken Cobb Salad

Preparation Time: 10 Minutes

Cooking Time: 10 Minutes

Servings: 4

Ingredients:

- 1/2 lb. Chicken, sliced
- ¼ tsp. Smoked Paprika
- 2 Eggs, hardboiled & chopped
- 2 tbsp. Olive Oil
- Salt & Pepper, as needed
- 4 Ham slices
- ¼ tsp. Onion Powder
- ½ of 1 Avocado, medium & sliced
- ½ cup Cucumbers, chopped
- 3 cups Greens of your choice
- ½ cup Cherry Tomatoes quartered

Directions:

1. First, marinate the chicken with salt, onion powder, pepper, and smoked paprika. Set it aside.
2. Heat a large cast-iron skillet over medium-low heat.
3. Stir in the chicken and sear it for 4 minutes on each side or until the chicken is cooked. Slice it once cooled.
4. Place all the remaining ingredients needed to make the salad along with the chicken.
5. Serve it with the dressing just before serving.

6. Enjoy.

Nutrition: Calories: 130Kcal Proteins: 5g Fiber: 4g Fat: 7g Carbohydrates: Sugar: 4g Sodium: 454mg

Cauliflower Pizza

Preparation Time: 10 Minutes

Cooking Time: 30 Minutes

Servings: 6

Ingredients:

- 1 Cauliflower head, medium & finely chopped
- 1 cup Mozzarella Cheese, grated
- 1 Egg, large & preferably farm-raised
- Salt & Pepper, to taste

Directions:

1. First, place the cauliflower chops in the food processor and process them until they are riced. Tip: Do not over process and puree it.
2. Next, transfer the riced cauliflower to a glass bowl and microwave them for 5 minutes or until they are soft.
3. After that, move the softened cauliflower to a clean tea towel and squeeze it well to remove all the moisture. Tip: It should not have any moisture as the pizza crust won't be crispy then.
4. Now, keep the squeezed cauliflower in a large-sized bowl and stir in the egg, grated cheese, and seasoning to it.
5. Combine well until you get a cauliflower dough.
6. Then, transfer the cauliflower 'dough' to a parchment-paper-lined baking sheet and spread it out evenly.

7. Apply olive oil over the cauliflower crust and bake at 180 C or 350 F for 14 minutes or until golden in color.

8. Finally, top it with toppings of your choice and garnish with more cheese.

9. Bake for further 5 minutes or until the cheese is gooey and bubbling.

10. Serve it hot.

Nutrition: Calories: 236Kcal Carbohydrates: 4g Fat: 15.5g Proteins: 17.8g

Sirloin Steak

Preparation Time: 10 Minutes

Cooking Time: 13 Minutes

Servings: 4

Ingredients:

- 4 × 8 oz. Sirloin Steak
- 1 tbsp. Butter, preferably
- grass-fed
- For the marinade:
- ¼ cup Coconut Aminos
- ½ tsp. Black Pepper
- ¼ cup Olive Oil
- 1 tsp. Sea Salt
- 2 tbsp. Balsamic Vinegar
- ½ tsp. Garlic Powder
- 1 tsp. Italian Seasoning

Directions:

1. First, marinate the steak with the marinade and allow it to marinate overnight if time permits.
2. Before cooking, thaw the meat about half an hour before.
3. Preheat the oven to 200 C or 400 F.
4. Meanwhile, heat a large cast-iron skillet over medium-high heat.
5. Now, spoon in the butter and melt it.

6. Then, place the steaks in a single layer in the skillet and sear them for 2 to 3 minutes per side or until they are browned with grill marks.
7. Next, transfer the skillet to the oven. Bake for 3 to 6 minutes or until it is cooked to your desired doneness.
8. Take the skillet from the oven. Allow it to cool for 5 minutes before slicing.
9. Serve it warm.

Nutrition: Calories: 475Kcal Carbohydrates: 5g Fat: 26g Fiber: 0g Saturated Fat: 9g Sugar: 1g Proteins: 49g Sodium: 554mg

Bacon-Wrapped Chicken

Preparation Time: 5 Minutes

Cooking Time: 20 Minutes

Servings: 4

Ingredients:

- 1 lb. Chicken Breast Tenderloin
- 8 Bacon Slices
- 4 Aged Cheddar Cheese Slices, sliced into two

Directions:

1. First, to make this easy chicken fare, pour water into a large mixing bowl filled with warm water and spoon in salt. Mix.
2. Next, place the chicken breast tenderloin in it and soak it for a minimum of 10 minutes.
3. Tip: The chicken should be immersed in it.
4. Preheat the oven to 230 C
5. Now, take out the chicken from the water and dry it up using a paper towel.
6. Then, make a slice in the middle of the chicken pieces and place the cheese slices.
7. After that, wrap the bacon over the stuffed chicken.
8. Once covered, arrange the chicken pieces on a greased parchment-paper-lined baking sheet.
9. Finally, bake for about 15minutes or until the chicken is cooked through.

10. When done, keep the chicken pieces under the broiler for 2 to 3 minutes to become crispier.

Nutrition: Calories: 301Kcal Carbohydrates: 1g Fat: 17g Proteins: 35g

Pork Tenderloin

Preparation Time: 10 Minutes

Cooking Time: 20 Minutes

Servings: 8

Ingredients:

- 1 lb. × 2 Pork Tenderloins
- ½ tsp. Oregano, dried
- 1 tbsp. Olive Oil
- 1 tbsp. Dijon Mustard
- For the sauce:
- 1 tsp. Tarragon
- ¼ tsp. Garlic Powder
- 2 tsp. Hot Horseradish
- 1 cup Chicken Stock
- Salt & Pepper, as required
- 1/3 cup Heavy Cream
- 1 tbsp. Dijon Mustard
- 1 tbsp. Butter, preferably grass-fed

Directions:

1. To begin with, slice each of the pork tenderloins into three pieces.
2. With the help of a meat mallet, pound the meat pieces until ½ thick. Place it in a large wide plate.
3. Now, spoon in olive oil, pepper, oregano, and Dijon mustard. Set it aside for 15 minutes.

4. In the meantime, place all the ingredients needed to make the sauce, excluding butter, in a frying pan.
5. Bring the sauce to a boil, then lower the heat. Simmer the mixture for 12 minutes or until thickened.
6. Off the heat and spoon in the butter to it. Whisk well.
7. Preheat the grill to high heat.
8. Arrange the pork pieces on high heat and grill for 4 minutes per side or until it is slightly pink inside.
9. Keep it aside for 5 minutes.
10. Serve it warm and drizzle the sauce over it. Enjoy.

Nutrition: Calories: 229Kcal Carbohydrates: 0.01g Fat: 11g Proteins: 24g

Rosemary Buttered Pork Chops

Preparation Time: 5 Minutes

Cooking Time: 20 Minutes

Servings: 4

Ingredients:

- ½ tbsp. olive oil
- 2 tbsp. butter
- 1 tbsp. rosemary
- Four pork chops
- Salt and black pepper to taste
- Pinch of paprika
- ½ tsp. chili powder

Directions:

3. Rub the pork chops with olive oil, salt, black pepper, paprika, and chili powder. Heat a grill to medium, add the pork chops and cook for 10 minutes, flipping once halfway through.
4. Remove to a serving plate. In a pan over low heat, warm the butter until it turns a nutty brown. Pour over the pork chops, sprinkle with rosemary, and serve.

Nutrition: Calories 363 Fat 21.4 g Carbs 3.8 g Protein 38.5 g

SOUP AND STEWS

Buffalo Chili

Preparation Time: 25 minutes

Cooking Time: 35 minutes

Servings: 8

Ingredients:

- Lb. Ground Buffalo
- Cans whole peeled tomatoes
- 8 C Beef stock
- 1 Medium White onion
- TBSP Cumin
- 1 TBSP Salt
- 1 TBSP Black pepper
- 2 Large Garlic cloves
- 1 TBSP Garlic powder
- 1 TBSP Onion powder
- ¼ C Chili powder

Directions:

1   Dice onion. In a large pot, brown meat with onion. Add all seasonings with a both cans of tomatoes and with your spoon give the tomatoes a rough chop. Simmer for 15 minutes then add the rest of the broth. Simmer

covered on low heat for 30 minutes or as long as you have time, stirring occasionally.

2   Serve with cornbread or Native Fry Bread.

Nutrition: 261 calories 5g fats 8g fiber

Mushroom and Leek Soup

Preparation Time: 10 minutes

Cooking Time: 30 minutes

Servings: 4

Ingredients:

- 1 tablespoon olive oil
- 1 large leek, sliced thin (white and light green parts only)
- 1 ½ pounds fresh sliced mushrooms
- 1 small white onion, chopped
- cloves minced garlic
- cups vegetable broth (divided)
- tablespoons arrowroot powder
- ¼ cup canned coconut milk
- 1 tablespoon fresh chopped thyme
- 1 tablespoon fresh chopped rosemary
- Salt and pepper, to taste

Directions:

1 Heat the oil in a large saucepan over medium heat. Add the leeks and cook for 4 to 5 minutes until just browned. Stir in the mushrooms, onion, and garlic and cook for 6 to 8 minutes until tender.

2 Pour in 2 tablespoons of the vegetable broth and scrape up the browned bits from the bottom of the pan. Stir in

the arrowroot powder then stir in the coconut milk and the rest of the broth.

3   Bring the mixture to a simmer then stir in the herbs, salt, and pepper. Simmer the soup, covered, for 15 to 20 minutes then serve hot.

Nutrition: 180 Calories 17g Carbs 9g Fat 5g Protein

Lamb and Root Vegetable Stew

Preparation Time: 15 minutes

Cooking Time: 30 minutes

Servings: 1

Ingredients:

- 1 tablespoon coconut oil
- large carrots, peeled and sliced
- medium turnips, peeled and sliced
- 1 large parsnip, peeled and sliced
- 1 large sweet potato, peeled and chopped
- 1 large yellow onion, chopped
- 1-pound lamb shank, chopped
- (14-ounce) cans diced tomatoes
- cups beef stock (low sodium)
- 1 teaspoon fresh chopped rosemary
- ½ teaspoon fresh chopped thyme
- Salt and pepper

Directions:

1   Heat the oil in a large saucepan over medium-high heat. Add the vegetables and cook for 4 to 5 minutes until lightly browned. Stir in the lamb along with the tomatoes, stock, and seasonings.
2   Bring the mixture to a boil then reduce heat and simmer, covered, for one hour – stir every 15 minutes. Uncover

the pot and simmer for another 45 minutes then serve hot.

Nutrition: 355 Calories 22g Carbs 19g Fat 25g Protein

Easy Chicken and Vegetable Soup

Preparation Time: 10 minutes

Cooking Time: 40 minutes

Servings: 6

Ingredients:

- 1 tablespoon olive oil
- cups cooked chicken breast, chopped
- 1 medium yellow onion, chopped
- 1 small leek, sliced thin (white and light green parts only)
- 8 cups low sodium chicken stock
- large carrots, peeled and sliced
- 1 medium zucchini, sliced
- 1 large stalk celery, sliced
- 1 red pepper, diced
- 1 cup diced tomatoes
- ¼ cup fresh chopped parsley
- 1 teaspoon fresh chopped thyme
- ½ teaspoon fresh chopped tarragon
- Salt and pepper

Directions:

1 Heat the oil in a large stockpot over medium heat. Add the chicken, onions, and leeks and cook for 4 to 5 minutes. Stir in the remaining ingredients and bring to a boil.

2 Reduce heat and simmer for 20 minutes until the vegetables are tender and the chicken heated through. Season with salt and pepper to taste and serve hot.

Nutrition: 157 Calories 24g Carbs 4g Fat 18g Protein

Spiced Pumpkin Soup

Preparation Time: 15 minutes

Cooking Time: 25 minutes

Servings: 6

Ingredients:

- 1 tablespoon butter
- 1 cup onion, chopped
- tablespoons coconut flour
- ½ teaspoon curry powder
- ¼ teaspoon cumin
- ¼ teaspoon ground nutmeg
- garlic cloves, crushed
- 1 cup peeled and cubed sweet potato
- ¼ teaspoon salt
- 14oz. cans of low sodium chicken broth
- 1 15oz. can of pumpkin
- 1 cup 1% milk
- 1 tablespoon fresh lime juice

Directions:

1 Heat 1 tablespoon oil in a large saucepan over medium heat. Melt butter in a Dutch oven or large saucepan over medium-high heat. Sauté onion for 3-4 minutes then add flour, curry, garlic, cumin and nutmeg and sauté for 1 minute.

2   Add sweet potato, salt, chicken broth and pumpkin and bring to a boil. Reduce heat to medium-low and simmer, partially covered for about 20-25 minutes or until sweet potatoes are cooked through and softened.

3   Remove from heat and let stand for 10 minutes to cool. Place half of the pumpkin mixture in a blender and process until smooth. Using a strainer, pour soup back into pan. Repeat with the rest of the soup. Raise heat to medium then stir in milk and cook for 5 minutes or until soup is heated through. Remove from heat and add lime juice.

Nutrition: 164 Calories 23g Carbs 5g Fat 10g Protein

Thai Coconut Vegetable Curry

Preparation Time: 15 minutes

Cooking Time: 25 minutes

Servings: 4

Ingredients:

- 1 tablespoon coconut oil
- 1 medium yellow onion, chopped
- 1 tablespoon fresh grated ginger
- 1 tablespoon fresh minced garlic
- 1 cup sliced carrots
- bell peppers, cored and chopped
- tablespoons Thai curry paste
- 1 (14-ounce) can coconut milk (full fat)
- ½ cup vegetable broth
- cups fresh chopped kale
- Salt, to taste

Directions:

1 Heat the oil in a large skillet over medium heat. Add the onion and cook until translucent – about 4 to 5 minutes. Stir in the ginger and garlic and cook for another 30 seconds.

2 Add the carrots and bell peppers – cook for 4 to 5 minutes until tender, stirring occasionally. Stir in the curry paste and cook for 2 minutes.

3   Add the coconut milk, vegetable broth, and kale then stir well. Bring to a boil then reduce heat and simmer for 5 to 10 minutes until the vegetables are tender – stir as needed. Season the curry with salt to taste and serve hot.

Nutrition: 187 Calories 24g Carbs 7g Fat 7g Protein

VEGETABLES

Tropical Mango and Lettuce Salad

Preparation Time: 15 minutes

Cooking Time: 5 minutes

Serving: 2

Ingredients:

- ½ of Romaine lettuce hand
- ½ of Blushed Butter Oak lettuce hand
- 1/3 cup of watercress
- green mangos
- 1 cucumber
- 1/3 cup of peanuts
- For the dressing:
- 1 small mango
- tablespoons of white wine vinegar
- teaspoons of Dijon mustard
- 1/4 cup of olive oil
- 1/3 cup of natural apple juice
- Salt and pepper as desired

Directions:

1 Wash the lettuces, watercress and cucumber and strain well (leave dry) Use a large salad bowl and combine the

Romaine and Butter Oak lettuce (shred them into the bowl with your hands) then add in the watercress leaves, set aside Peel the mangos and cut each mango length wise on each side (top & bottom) discard the seed in the middle, and then dice the mangos in small dices. Put in a small bowl Take the cucumber and cut off both ends. Run a fork lengthwise all around the cucumber then cut it in half (lengthwise) use a small spoon and scrape out and discard the seeds. Slice the cucumber in half and then cut slices crosswise (it's nice if the sizes of the cucumber are around the same sizes of the mango dices) pour the cucumbers in the bowl with the mangos. To make the dressing: peel and de-seed the mango puree it with a blender or food processor and then pass it through a colander. Pour the strained mango in a blender and add in the vinegar (or vinegar and lime juice) 2 teaspoons of Dijon mustard, olive oil and apple juice. Blend until smooth then season with salt and pepper as desired. Add the mango and cucumber to the lettuce bowl and mix then pour in the dressing and toss or mix around. Add in the peanuts and toss or mix again.

Nutrition: 108 calories 2g fiber 14g carbs

Pancetta Pear and Arugula

Preparation Time: 15 minutes

Cooking Time: 5 minutes

Servings: 2

Ingredients:

- For salad:
- cups baby arugula
- tablespoon olive oil
- oz thinly sliced pancetta
- firm-ripe pears
- For vinaigrette:
- 1/2 tablespoon fresh lemon juice
- 1 tablespoon mild honey
- 1 tablespoon Champagne vinegar
- 1/8 teaspoon ground black pepper
- tablespoons olive oil
- 1/8 teaspoon salt

Directions:

1   Use a salad bowl and whisk the lemon juice, mild honey, champagne vinegar, pepper and salt. Pour in the olive oil a spoon at a time whisking between each spoon until everything is well combined. Place a heavy skillet over medium heat and cook the pancetta in oil, turning it over often, until it gets crisp (this should take about 4 to 6 minutes)

2   Place the cooked pancetta on paper towels to drain out the oil, the pancetta will crisp once crisp chop it into bite-sized piece Wash, dry, and core the pears, cut them lengthwise into slices that are about ¼ of an inch thick. Add the arugula to the salad bowl with sauce and toss, add in the pears, cheese and pancetta toss a bit more. Serve the salad.

Nutrition: 119 calories 16g carbs 3g protein

Veggie and Eggs Salad

Preparation Time: 10 minutes

Cooking Time: 10 minutes

Servings: 4

Ingredients:

- 1 avocado, pitted, peeled and chopped
- 1 small red onion, chopped
- eggs
- 1 small red bell pepper, chopped
- ¼ cup homemade mayonnaise
- A pinch of sea salt
- Black pepper to taste
- 1 tablespoon lemon juice

Directions:

1. Put eggs in a large saucepan, add water to cover, place on stove over medium-high heat, bring to a boil, reduce heat to low and cook for 10 minutes.
2. Drain eggs, leave them in cold water to cool down, peel, chop them and put in a salad bowl.
3. Add a pinch of sea salt and pepper to taste, onion, bell pepper, avocado, lemon juice and mayo, toss to coat and serve right away.

Nutrition: 240 calories 19.2g fat 4g fiber

Tomato and Pear Bowl

Preparation Time: 10 minutes

Cooking Time: 0 minute

Servings: 4

Ingredients:

- 1 pear, sliced
- cups lettuce leaves, torn
- 1 small cucumber, chopped
- ½ cup cherry tomatoes, cut in halves
- ½ cup red grapes, cut in halves
- A pinch of sea salt
- Black pepper to taste
- tablespoons orange juice
- ¼ cup extra virgin olive oil
- 1 tablespoon orange zest, grated
- 1 tablespoon parsley, minced

Directions:

1 In a bowl, mix all the ingredients, toss, divide between plates and serve.

Nutrition: 174 calories 12.9g fat 16.2g carbs

Apricot Sausage Kabobs

Preparation Time: 10 minutes

Cooking Time: 15 minutes

Servings: 4

Ingredients

- 3/4 cup apricot preserves
- 3/4 cup Dijon mustard
- 1-pound Johnsonville® Fully Cooked Polish Kielbasa Sausage Rope, cut into 12 pieces
- 12 dried apricots
- 12 medium fresh mushrooms

Direction

1   Stir together preserves and mustard in a small bowl. Set aside 1/2 cup for serving later. Alternately skewer sausage, mushrooms, and apricots on four metal or water-soaked wooden skewers. Cook in a covered grill at indirect heat, turning and basting often with the remaining sauce, for 15-20 minutes, or until meat juices are clear. Heat up the reserved sauce and serve warm with the kabobs and rice.

Nutrition: 617 Calories: 4g fiber 60g carbohydrate 20g protein.

SNACK AND DESSERTS

Coleslaw with Avocado Dressing

Preparation Time: 15 Minutes

Cooking Time: 0 Minutes

Servings: 6

Ingredients:

- One small head green cabbage, sliced thin
- ½ cup shredded red cabbage
- One small red pepper, diced
- 1 cup avocado oil
- 1 large egg, beaten
- Juice from 1 lime
- 1 clove garlic, minced
- Salt to taste

Directions:

1. Combine the shredded cabbages with the red peppers in a bowl.
2. Place the avocado oil, egg, lime juice, and garlic in a blender.
3. Blend smooth, then season with salt to taste.
4. Toss the dressing with the salad and chill until ready to serve.

Nutrition: Calories 100 Fat, 6g Protein, 3g Net Carbs 6g

Creamsicle Fat Bombs

Preparation Time: 5 Minutes

Cooking Time: 0 Minutes

Servings: 10

Ingredients:

- 4 ounces cream cheese, softened
- ½ cup heavy cream
- ½ cup of coconut oil
- One teaspoon orange extract
- 8 to 12 drops liquid stevia extract

Directions:

1. Combine the cream cheese, heavy cream, and coconut oil in a bowl.
2. Blend with an immersion blender until smooth – microwave if needed to soften.
3. Stir in the orange extract and liquid stevia.
4. Spoon the mixture into silicone molds and freeze for 3 hours until solid.
5. Remove the fat bombs from the mold and store them in the freezer.

Nutrition: Calories 155 Fat 17g Protein 1g Net Carbs 0.5g

Baked Cauliflower Bites

Preparation Time: 15 Minutes

Cooking Time: 25 Minutes

Servings: 4

Ingredients:

- One small head cauliflower, chopped
- ¼ cup coconut flour
- Two large eggs
- ½ teaspoon garlic powder
- ¼ teaspoon onion powder
- Salt and pepper to taste

Directions:

1. Preheat the oven to 400 F
2. Place the cauliflower in a saucepan, then cover with water.
3. Boil until the cauliflower is tender, then drain and place in a food processor.
4. Pulse into rice-like grains, then pulse in the rest of the ingredients.
5. Drop the combination onto the baking sheet in a rounded spoonful.
6. Bake for 20 to 25 minutes or wait until browned, flipping once halfway through.

Nutrition: Calories 100 Fat 4.5g Protein 6g Net Carbs 4g

Bacon-Wrapped Shrimp

Preparation Time: 10 Minutes

Cooking Time: 15 Minutes

Servings: 4

Ingredients:

- Six slices of uncooked bacon
- Salt and pepper
- 12 large shrimp, peeled and deveined
- Paprika to taste

Directions:

1. Preheat the oven to 425 F
2. Cut the bacon in half, then wrap one piece around each shrimp.
3. Place the shrimp on the baking sheet and sprinkle with paprika, salt, and pepper.
4. Spray lightly with cooking spray, then bake for 15 minutes until bacon is crisp.

Nutrition: Calories 100 Fat 6g Protein 9g Net Carbs 0.5g

Raspberry Cheesecake Fluff

Preparation Time: 5 Minutes

Cooking Time: 0 Minutes

Servings: 4

Ingredients:

- 1 cup heavy (whipping) cream
- 8 ounces cream cheese, at room temperature
- 4 ounces raspberries
- ½ cup sugar substitute (such as Swerve)
- One teaspoon vanilla extract
- Pinch salt

Directions:

1. In a blender or a bowl using a hand mixer, whip the cream to stiff peaks, 2 to 4 minutes.
2. Add the cream cheese, raspberries, sugar substitute, vanilla, salt, and blend until smooth and well combined.

Nutrition: Calories: 417 Total Fat: 41g Protein: 5g Total Carbs: 7g Cholesterol: 143mg

Hot Fudge

Preparation Time: 5 Minutes

Cooking Time: 10 Minutes

Servings: 10

Ingredients:

- ½ cup (1 stick) salted butter
- 4 ounces dark chocolate (85% or higher)
- Two tablespoons unsweetened cocoa powder
- 1 cup sugar substitute (such as Swerve)
- 1 cup heavy (whipping) cream
- Two teaspoons vanilla extract
- Pinch salt

Directions:

1. In a saucepan, dissolve the butter and chocolate. Add the cocoa powder and sweetener, and whisk until the powder and sweetener dissolve 3 to 5 minutes.
2. Add the cream and bring to a boil, stirring constantly. Reduce the heat to low, and add the vanilla and salt.
3. Remove from the heat, let rest for 5 minutes, and serve hot over your favorite dessert.

Nutrition: Calories: 237 Total Fat: 24g Protein: 2g Total Carbs: 5g Fiber: 2g Cholesterol: 57mg

Hot Caramel Sauce

Preparation Time: 5 Minutes

Cooking Time: 10 Minutes

Servings: 8

Ingredients:

- ½ cup (1 stick) salted butter
- ¼ cup sugar substitute (such as Swerve)
- 1 cup heavy (whipping) cream
- ¼ to ½ teaspoon xanthan gum
- ½ teaspoon salt

Directions:

1. In a large saucepan over medium-low heat, dissolve the butter. Whisk in the sugar substitute until it is dissolved and incorporated, 3 to 5 minutes.
2. Add the cream, xanthan gum, and salt to the mixture, whisking continuously. Bring to a boil and let boil for 1 minute, then remove from the heat.
3. Serve hot.

Nutrition: Calories: 202 Total Fat: 22g Protein: 1g Total Carbs: 1g Cholesterol: 71mg

5-Minute Chocolate Mousse

Preparation Time: 5 Minutes

Cooking Time: 0 Minutes

Servings: 4

Ingredients:

- 1 (14-ounce) can coconut cream, chilled
- Three tablespoons unsweetened cocoa powder
- ¼ cup sugar substitute (such as Swerve)
- One teaspoon vanilla extract

Directions:

1. In a large mixing bowl, lash the coconut cream with a hand mixer until fluffy, about 3 minutes. If you don't have a hand mixer, you can whip it in the blender.
2. Fold in the cocoa powder, sugar substitute, and vanilla and serve immediately.

Nutrition: Calories: 222 Total Fat: 22g Protein: 1g Total Carbs: 5g Cholesterol: 0mg

Pumpkin Mousse

Preparation Time: 10 Minutes

Cooking Time: 30 Minutes

Servings: 4

Ingredients:

- 8 ounces cream cheese, at room temperature
- 1 cup canned pumpkin purée
- 1 cup heavy (whipping) cream
- Two tablespoons sugar substitute (such as Swerve)
- One teaspoon vanilla extract
- One teaspoon pumpkin pie spice
- ½ teaspoon ground cinnamon

Directions:

1. In a large mixer or a large bowl with a hand mixer, cream together the cream cheese and pumpkin until smooth, 1 to 2 minutes. If you don't have either type of mixer, you can use a blender.
2. Add the cream, sweetener, vanilla, pumpkin pie spice, and cinnamon. Mix it on high for 3 to 5 minutes, or until fluffy.
3. Chill for 30 minutes before serving.

Nutrition: Calories: 419 Total Fat: 41g Protein: 6g Total Carbs: 9g Cholesterol: 144mg

Snickerdoodle Mug Cake

Preparation Time: 5 Minutes

Cooking Time: 2 Minutes

Servings: 2

Ingredients:

- Two tablespoons salted butter
- Two tablespoons sugar substitute (such as Swerve)
- Two tablespoons almond flour
- Two tablespoons heavy (whipping) cream or coconut cream
- 1 large egg
- One teaspoon ground cinnamon, plus more for serving
- ½ teaspoon vanilla extract
- ½ teaspoon baking powder
- ¼ teaspoon cream of tartar
- ¼ teaspoon salt (optional)
- Cinnamon, for sprinkling

Directions:

1. In a coffee mug or glass measuring cup, microwave the butter until melted, about 30 seconds. Add the sugar substitute and stir vigorously with a fork. Add the almond flour, cream, egg, cinnamon, vanilla, baking powder, tartar, salt (if using), and mix until everything is combined.

2. Microwave for 50 to 70 seconds, or until the middle of the cake is moist; careful not to overcook.
3. Sprinkle with cinnamon and serve.

Nutrition: Calories: 229 Total Fat,: 23g Protein: 5g Total Carbs: 2g Cholesterol: 145mg

CPSIA information can be obtained
at www.ICGtesting.com
Printed in the USA
BVHW061923220321
603177BV00010B/878